101 Coolest T̶h̶i̶n̶g̶s̶ Do in London

Introduction

So you're going to London, huh? You lucky lucky thing! You are sure in for a treat because London is one of the most dynamic and exciting cities on this planet. There's a mix of incredible green spaces, cultural centres, world-class festivals, and delicious food and drink that makes London one of the most enduringly popular tourist destinations on the face of the earth.

In this guide, we'll be giving you the low down on:
- the very best things to shove in your pie hole, whether that's a cup of traditional jellied eels, or the best places to sample authentic British beers
- the best shopping so that you can take a little piece of London back home with you, whether that's from an antiques market or a fancy department store
- incredible festivals, from partying on the streets of Notting Hill for carnival to chowing down at a London food festival
- the most thrilling outdoor activities, such as sliding down the world's tallest slide tunnel, and scaling the roof of a huge concert arena
- the coolest historical and cultural sights that you simply cannot afford to miss like watching the Changing of the Guard, and visiting ancient castles on the outskirts of the city

- where to party like someone a true Londoner and get down with the locals

- and tonnes more coolness besides!

Let's not waste any more time – here are the 101 coolest things not to miss in London!

1. Get Really Local With a Cup of Jellied Eels

To tell the truth, London is not a city where you will probably encounter all that much traditional British food as the Brits love cuisines from all over the world, but if you want to try some food that has London right at its heart, jellied eels are the way to go. Unfortunately, that's not a euphemism for something altogether more palatable, and we are literally talking about cold eels in fishy jelly here. But it's an East End staple, and if you want to try it for yourself, you can chow down on jellied eels at Eel Pie House in Leytonstone. *(481A High Rd Leytonstone)*

2. Get Your Photo Taken in a Red Phone Booth

The red phone booth is something really iconic that you can find on the streets of London, even though everyone has a mobile phone these days and they are hardly ever used. But this means that you won't be jostling for competition to get inside the booth to take the perfect red phone "yes, I'm in London" selfie.

3. Enjoy the Best Indian Food Outside of India on Brick Lane

The UK and India has a long history. Of course, India used to be a British colony, and in the 1950s and 1960s when there was a labour shortage in the UK, the British invited many Indians to the UK to work. As a result of this immigration, Indian food became immensely popular in the country, and you can find curry houses in every corner of the capital. But if you are really serious about curry, paying a trip to Brick Lane in the East End is an absolute must. This is a whole street full of curry houses, mainly serving Bengali food, and the smells and tastes are incredible.

4. Hang Out With Hipsters at Dalston Superstore

Dalston Superstore hasn't been open for all that long, but its effect on the East End has been incredible. As soon as this gay bar/club/café/event space opened in Dalston's East End, this neighbourhood suddenly transformed from a place with grubby backstreets and dive bars to the most happening, artsy address in the capital. This is most definitely a hipster haunt, and weekend parties are when you can experience this at its height. But if you don't want to go full tilt hipster, they also serve a lovely brunch in the daytime.

(117 Kingsland High Street; http://dalstonsuperstore.com)

5. Get Lost in the Hampton Court Palace Maze

For history buffs on a visit to London, Hampton Court Palace, a Royal palace that dates back to the 16th century is a must visit. But this is more than just a palace with stately apartments to peruse. In fact, probably the most famous aspect of the palace is its garden maze. The maze was commissioned by William III in 1700, and it's very hard to traverse with its twists, turns, and dead ends. Kids will be entranced by it.

(www.hrp.org.uk/hampton-court-palace)

6. Sample Lots of Deliciousness at Borough Market

London does not have a reputation as a foodie city, but honestly, this is unfair, and you can find this out for yourself on a trip to incredible Borough Market on the Southbank. Borough Market is often considered to be the best food market in all of London, and with 1000 years of history behind it, who could possibly disagree? Anything and everything is on offer at this outdoor hub of deliciousness, and the best thing is that the vendors are very liberal with their food samples.

(8 Southwark St; http://boroughmarket.org.uk)

7. Take a Dip at Hampstead Ponds

Okay, we know that London summertime might last for all of a couple of months (if that) but if you do find yourself on a warm and sunny day in the capital, there is no better way of cooling off than taking a dip in the refreshing waters of Hampstead Ponds on Hampstead Heath. There are three ponds on the fields: one for guys, one for girls, and one for everyone, so no matter your persuasion you can feel perfectly comfortable, and enjoy the views of Hampstead around you while in the water.

8. Enjoy the View and a Drink on Dalston Roof Park

When spring appears in London, suddenly all the rooftops around the city turn into bars, clubs, and hangout spaces. This is an incredible way to enjoy the warmer months in the capital, and to enjoy the most spectacular views over London. One of our favourite rooftop spaces has to be the Dalston Roof Park. The Roof Park is the only rooftop garden in this area, so you get to check out the vista of the East End. And there are often live music acts playing, DJs spinning tunes, or even rooftop yoga classes.

(18 Ashwin St; www.bootstrapcompany.co.uk)

9. Catch some Contemporary Dance at Sadler's Wells

Without a shadow of a doubt, London is one of the cultural centres of the world, and you'll find everything from dance to visual arts to jazz and everything in between. If dance is what does it for you, Sadler's Wells in the city centre is a theatre dedicated to this art form, with a leaning towards contemporary art forms, but you can also catch ballets here. Dance lovers need to keep up to date with their programme of events.

(Rosebury Avenue, www.sadlerswells.com)

10. Eat Duck and Waffle at, errr, Duck & Waffle

If comfort food is what gets you going, you need to know about Duck & Waffle restaurant which serves up, well, duck and waffle. Duck & Waffle has a lot going for it. It's open 24 hours a day so you can always get your fix, it's located 40 floors up so you get an incredible view of the whole city, and last but certainly not least, the food is just awesome. Of course, the duck and waffle is the highlight of the menu with confit duck leg, a fried duck egg, and glugs of maple syrup.

(110 Bishopsgate (Heron Tower), Heron Tower, 110 Bishopsgate, 38th Floor; https://duckandwaffle.com)

11. Go Ice Skating in Front of Somerset House

Although many people choose to visit London in the summer months, when the local population tends to be more cheerful and there are more daylight hours, we think that London does Christmas festivities very well indeed. If you find yourself in the English capital in the run up to Christmas and you are looking for a fun activity, you should know that there are pop-up ice skating rinks all over London during this time, and the loveliest of them all is perched directly in front of Somerset House, a stunning Neoclassical building that overlooks the River Thames.

(Strand WC2, www.somersethouse.org.uk)

12. Get Crafty at Drink, Shop & Do

If you are not much of a drinker, you might find yourself at a bit of a loss in the evening times of London, because the city's social life revolves firmly around the pub. But for an alternative evening and a chance to try something new, there's an awesome café in King's Cross called Drink, Shop & Do that you need to know about. This café is most famous and beloved for its awesome evening classes, workshops, and activities. How about a Dance Like Beyonce class? Or what about creating your own unicorn shaped piñata? There's all this and more and this cool hangout.

(9 Caledonian Rd, Kings Cross; http://drinkshopdo.com)

13. Walk the Canals of London

The most famous city in the world for canals is, of course, Venice, but if you want to feel the serenity of walking along canals, London is also a fantastic city. In fact, there's more than 100km of canals across the city, and many have walkable paths alongside them. Walking along Regent's Canal is particularly popular, and there is a well trodden route that will take you from picturesque Little Venice, past Regent's Park, and finally to Camden.

14. Get Your Fill of Modern Art at the Tate

If you are an artsy kind of person, you can truly fill your boots while in London because this city is absolutely bursting full of incredible galleries. While there are many art spaces to choose from, the Tate Modern is probably the most impressive of all the London galleries. You can find it within a disused power station on the Southbank, and the sheer scale of the place is breath taking. What's more, the permanent collection is totally free to peruse so this makes for a cheap afternoon out.

(Bankside SE1, www.tate.org.uk/visit/tate-modern)

15. Learn Something at LSE

The London School of Economics is one of the most acclaimed places for learning in the entire world, and the good news is that you don't have to sign up to a course to get a slice of the learning action. In fact, LSE hosts free lectures on almost every night of the week, inviting academics in all kinds of fields to talk about their particular areas of expertise. Whether you want to learn something about genetic engineering or moral philosophy, there is bound to be something that appeals.

(Houghton St, www.lse.ac.uk/home.aspx)

16. Get Decadent With Afternoon Tea at the Ritz

Afternoon tea is something quintessentially British, and you can't leave London without experiencing this at least once, and without a doubt, the very best place for a decadent afternoon tea is at the Ritz hotel. Their afternoon tea is hosted in the Palm Court, which is full of opulent chandeliers, marble towers, and palm trees. And the lunch itself is just as special with a selection of finger sandwiches, scones and pastries, endless tea, and even champagne. *(150 Piccadilly, St. James's; www.theritzlondon.com)*

17. Watch the Changing of the Guards

London is a city that has a lot of tradition and yet is progressive at the same time. If you want to get to grips with traditional London, watching the Changing of the Guards outside of Buckingham Palace is an experience that you cannot afford to miss. This ceremony takes place at 11:30am each day, and it's totally free to act this historic ceremony, which is full of British pomp and pageantry.

18. Pay Your Respects at the Diana Memorial

Princess Diana was, of course, one of the most beloved members of the Royal family to have ever lived. If you wish to remember the Princess and pay your respects to her life, you can visit the Princess Diana Memorial Fountain in Hyde Park. The monument is made from 545 pieces of stunning Cornish granite, which have been pieced together using traditional skills. It's possible to walk right to the centre of the fountain, the design reflecting the openness of Diana's life.

19. Take in the View From the London Eye

London is a very beautiful city, but it's even more so when you manage to take in the city from a height. And what better way of doing so than by taking a ride on the London Eye? At the time that the giant Ferris Wheel was constructed, it was the tallest Ferris wheel in the whole world with a height of 135 metres. As you reach the highest point in the capsule, you can take in the whole city, from the business district of Canary Wharf to the stunning buildings of the Houses of Parliament.

(www.londoneye.com)

20. Go Boating in Victoria Park

One of the loveliest things about London is that although it's a busy and dynamic city, it's also a wonderful place for relaxing with its incredible selection of parks and green spaces. One of the most beloved of these spaces has to be Victoria Park in Tower Hamlets. As well as offering ample amounts of space for walking or jogging, there is also a lake in the centre of the park where you can actually rent boats and pass a pleasant hour on the calm water.

21. Tuck Into Cheap Vietnamese Food in East London

We're gonna be straight with you – London isn't always the cheapest city for a vacation, particularly if you enjoy eating out a lot. But there are certainly some cheap eats to be found in London, and if you enjoy Vietnamese food, waste no time and head straight to Shoreditch. On Kingsland Road, you can find an abundance of authentic and super cheap Vietnamese canteens. Many of these places sell a big bowl of pho for about £5, and you can bring your own bottle of booze to most of them too.

22. Take in a Concert at Union Chapel

London is a historic city, and this means that you can find stunning churches from many centuries ago in virtually any neighbourhood you might find yourself in. Union Chapel is a very pretty church in the fancy Islington neighbourhood, but it's more than just pretty to look at, because Union Chapel also hosts regular concerts. You can find both traditional church recitals as well as contemporary live music there, so it's worth checking out their programme of events.

(Union Chapel, Compton Terrace; www.unionchapel.org.uk)

23. Dance Til You Drop at Ministry of Sound

London is a city that has an extremely youthful energy, and this means that there are plenty of nightclubs catering to all music tastes in every borough of the city. But there is one club that's a cut above the rest, and that's Ministry of Sound. If you are really serious about dance music, this is the place that attracts the best DJ talent, as well as around 300,000 dance fanatics every year.

(103 Gaunt Street, www.ministryofsound.com)

24. Get Lost in Ancient History at the British Museum

London is a museum lover's paradise. While you could easily spend a whole vacation making your way from one museum to another, if you only have time to fit one museum into your schedule, make sure that it's the British Museum. The history of this museum dates right back to the 18th century, and its exhibitions relating to ancient history are particularly impressive. Some special artefacts include a gold bowl from

Sicily, dated to 600 BC, and a beaded necklace from Scotland that dates to 3000 BC.

(Great Russell St, www.britishmuseum.org)

25. Wave a Rainbow Flag at London Pride

London is one of the most gay friendly cities on this planet, and LGBT visitors to the city are sure to have a whale of a time at the selection of gay bars and clubs. The pinnacle of London's gay year, however, has to be the annual Gay Pride, which typically takes place each year in July. There are many events that take place throughout Pride week, but the highlight is a colourful parade on the Saturday, which is followed by a live concert in Trafalgar Square

(http://prideinlondon.org)

26. Chow Down on the Best Steak in London

We know that you probably haven't ventured all the way to London to eat steak, but who can say no to a delicious steak dinner? Very few people, and that's why you need to know about the best steak restaurant in the whole of the capital, Foxlow, which has a few locations around the city. As this is a Mediterranean restaurant, you can expect dishes that are somewhat more exciting than steak and chips, but it's always the meat that steals the show.

(69-73 St John St; www.foxlow.co.uk)

27. Watch a Radical Play at the Royal Court

London is an incredible creative hub, and if you have any interest in the arts, your trip to London will surely be one to remember for a lifetime. One of our favourite creative centres in the city is the Royal Court Theatre in Sloane Square, a theatre that is dedicated to showcasing the works of new writers. The theatre is credited with showcasing the first works of writers and practitioners who are now big names in theatre, such as Sarah Kane and Martin Crimp. Tickets are just £10 on Mondays!

(Sloane Square; https://royalcourttheatre.com)

28. Treat Yourself to a Cupcake at Peggy Porschen Cakes

Although mainland Europe gets more credit for its baking prowess than the UK, we think that the bakeries across London are second to none, which is very good news indeed for cupcake fanatics. Peggy Porschen Cakes is a chic bakery in the posh neighbourhood of Belgravia where the cakes are nothing short of incredible. Honestly, nothing that you buy here is going to be bad, but the banoffee cupcake with its gooey toffee centre is something extra special.

(116 Ebury St, Belgravia; www.peggyporschen.com)

29. Catch The Proms at the Royal Albert Hall

London has no shortage of incredible concert venues, but the Royal Albert Hall might just be the grandest and most impressive of them all. Located in the fancy neighbourhood of Kensington, the Royal Albert Hall has played host to performers like Shirley Bassey and Tony Bennett. But the highlight of their calendar of events has to be The Proms. In the summertime, there are more than 1000 classical performances in London as part of the Proms, and many of the grandest are at the Royal Albert Hall.

(Kensington Grove; www.royalalberthall.com)

30. Tuck Into Cheap Eats at Pop Brixton

Pop Brixton is a relatively new addition to London's gastronomic scene, but a very welcome one, because it offers incredible variety and unbeatable value. The basic idea is that there's a variety of vendors, and a communal seating area where everyone sits together and chows down. There are street food prices here, but the quality is incredible, so whether you'd prefer Vietnamese rolls or curry goat, the choice is yours.

(49 Brixton Station Road; www.popbrixton.org)

31. Have a Day of Learning at the London Transport Museum

London has one of the most iconic transport systems in the world, with its bright red double decker buses and its underground Tube system. But how much do you actually know about London's transport? The London Transport Museum is the place to go for a complete education. Inside the building, the highlight is the many old vehicles on display, such as old trams, buses, rail carriages, and trolleybuses.

(Covent Garden Piazza; www.ltmuseum.co.uk)

32. Party in Victoria Park at Lovebox

When the sun shines on London in the summer months, the local Brits want to spend as much time in that sunshine as possible, and there are many weekend festivals that give you the opportunity to do just that. Lovebox is hosted in Victoria

Park every July, and it has a reputation for being a cool and yet accessible, and since there is no overnight camping, you don't have to worry about that. Acts that have performed at Lovebox in the past include Goldfrapp and Mark Ronson. *(http://loveboxfestival.com)*

33. Fill Your Stomach at the Taste of London

While London doesn't have the best reputation as a culinary city, this is totally unfair as there are many gastronomic treats to be found, and you can sample many of these at the annual Taste of London event. This restaurant festival showcases the very best of London's dining scene across four days in November without the high restaurant prices. As well as lots of deliciousness to eat, you'll find gourmet shopping, and masterclasses from some of Britain's top chefs. *(http://london.tastefestivals.com)*

34. Drink in a Speakeasy, Mayor of Scaredy Cat Town

If you find yourself in London on a Friday night and you just can't decide where you should go for a cocktail or two, allow us to point you in the direction of Mayor of Scaredy Cat

Town, a speakeasy style bar located in the trendy Spitalfields area. Inside, you can expect dimly lit interiors, wooden tables and high stools. In other words, it's the perfect date place. And the cocktails, like the margarita with lemongrass, are more than a bit special.

(12-16 Artillery Ln; www.themayorofscaredycattown.com)

35. Go Deer Spotting in Richmond Park

If you have the time in London, be sure to venture to the outer stretches of the city. This can be particularly rewarding if you are outdoorsy because this is where many of the city's best green spaces exist. Take Richmond Park, for example. With 2500 acres of land, it's three times as large as New York's Central Park. The really special thing about this deer is that large numbers of red deer and fallow deer roam free there, and autumn mornings are a great time to spot them.

(www.royalparks.org.uk/parks/richmond-park)

36. Watch the Opening of Tower Bridge

London is bursting full of famous bridges, but Tower Bridge might just be the most iconic of them all. Because there is actually a lot of boat traffic on the River Thames, you have the chance to see the bridge open. There are no set times when the bridge actually opens, but it does open on average 17 times per day. This means you should grab a hot cup of coffee and sit on the Southbank while you wait for one of the most spectacular bridges in the world to open for a passing ship.

(Tower Bridge Road SE1; www.towerbridge.org.uk)

37. Devour a Luxurious Lobster Roll From Smack Deli

When you're on holiday, it's most definitely a time when you are allowed to indulge in a way that you might not do so at home. But this doesn't mean that you have to spend loads of cash on fancy hotels. For us, we can't think of anything that's much more decadent than the lobster rolls served at Smack Deli in Mayfair, London's poshest area. They serve up soft and buttery brioche rolls that are crammed full of tender lobster, and deli lunches don't get much better than that in our opinion.

(Kemble House, 58 Dean St, Soho; http://smacklobster.com)

38. Get Back to Nature in Epping Forest

If you are outdoorsy and you are worried about a capital city like London being too oppressive for you, you can think again. If you venture out into the suburbs, you can find the most incredible green spaces and areas of woodland. Epping Forest, for example, is almost 2500 hectares of woodland, heath, rivers, grassland, bogs and ponds. Of course, this is a spectacular spot for a long weekend hike, and the forest also attracts a large number of mountain bikers.

39. Find Some Zen at the Kyoto Japanese Garden in Holland Park

Although London is an extremely fun city to visit, there might be some times when you feel as though you need to escape the hustle and bustle. When that moment comes, all you need to do is head over to Holland Park to find the Kyoto Japanese Garden. This garden was donated to London by the Kyoto Chamber of Commerce in 1991, and it includes stone lanterns, tiered waterfalls, and colourful fish swimming around.

40. Look at Original Beatles Lyrics at the British Library

If you think of yourself as a culture vulture, the British Library in Central London needs to be on your London hit-list. This is no ordinary library. The British Library is the official national library, and it's the largest library in the whole world by number of items catalogued. Of course, this means that there are many treasures to be explored, but a highlight for all music fans has to be original Beatles lyrics on display, hand written by John Lennon himself.

(96 Euston Rd, Kings Cross; www.bl.uk)

41. Take a Dip in the London Fields Lido

If you are a water baby and you love to swim, there's actually quite a few lovely places in London where you can take a dip. One of the best of these has to be London Fields Lido in the East End. This Olympic size swimming pool is an outdoor pool, but fear not because it's heated right throughout the year. There is also a sundeck and a café, so whether you want to get in a good swim or you just want to relax, this could be the place.

(www.hackney.gov.uk/ london-fields-lido)

42. Discover Contemporary Art at the Saatchi Gallery

If you are something of an art buff, there's a tonne of galleries around the city that you can visit. But if your tastes are firmly rooted in cutting edge contemporary art, we have to recommend a trip to the Saatchi Gallery, founded by advertising mogul and art collector Charles Saatchi. This gallery is credited with launching the careers of many iconic British visual artists, including Tracey Emin and Damien Hirst. You can find the gallery in the fancy Sloane Square area.

(Duke Of York's HQ, King's Rd, Chelsea; www.saatchigallery.com)

43. Slide Down World's Largest Slide Tunnel

If you fancy yourself as something of an adventurer, and you prefer doing this to ambling from museum to museum, one of the greatest things that you can do is take a ride on The Slide, which is the world's tallest and longest tunnel slide with a height of 178 metres. Your trip down the slide will take a total of 40 seconds, and in this time you'll be taken round sharp turns, and you'll end with a 50 metre straight finish as you crash to the ground.

(Queen Elizabeth Olympic Park, Stratford;
http://arcelormittalorbit.com/whats-on/the-slide)

44. Discover How British Rooms Have Changed at the Geffrye Museum

The Geffrye Museum is one of the hidden gems of both London's museum scene and of Hackney. Located within a beautiful 18th century almshouse, the Geffrye Museum takes its visitors on a journey through British rooms since the 17th century. The selection of period rooms includes a hall from 1630, a parlour from 1745, a living room from 1930, and even a loft style apartment from 1998. On a sunny day, it's also a treat to walk around the museum's very own herb garden. *(136 Kingsland Rd; www.geffrye-museum.org.uk)*

45. Watch the Fireworks at Alexandra Palace

Guy Fawkes Night is a UK specific celebration that's a whole lot of fun, and as good a reason as any to make a trip to London at the beginning of November. This day is a commemoration of the Gunpowder Plot, and the locals celebrate with huge bonfires and epic fireworks displays. These can be found in virtually every park in the city on November 5th, but we particularly love the fireworks show at the stunning Alexandra Palace in north London. *(Alexandra Palace Way N22; www.alexandrapalace.com)*

46. Have a Ukelele Jam at the Queen of Hoxton

If you think of yourself as a musical person, you can do one better than getting some gig tickets while you're in London, and actually join in with the music making. The Queen of Hoxton is an awesome bar with fantastic events in the East End, and each Monday evening they have a ukulele jam session. They provide the instruments so all you need to do is show up and show off your musical prowess.

(1 Curtain Road; http://queenofhoxton.com)

47. Enjoy the Beer Garden of the Edinboro Castle

Brits sure do love a pint of beer, and never more so than on a sunny day. This is when the beer gardens of pubs around the city will open up and people will drink pints of lager, cider, and gin and tonics in the outdoors. One of the loveliest beer gardens in the city has to be at The Edinboro Castle, a pub that you can find in Camden. With enough seating space for 300 people, this is the place to make some British friends on a sunny London day.

(57 Mornington Terrace; www.edinborocastlepub.co.uk)

48. Have a Day of Decadent Shopping at Harrods

If your idea of the perfect getaway is having the opportunity to max out your credit card and buy some truly special things, London is not a city that will disappoint you in the slightest. The shopping in virtually every neighbourhood is second to none, but there is one iconic department store that is famous around the world and towers above the rest. It is, of course, Harrods. Located in Knightsbridge, Harrods sells everything under the sun, but always to the highest quality, and it's the perfect spot for some indulgent souvenir shopping.

(87-135 Brompton Rd, Knightsbridge; www.harrods.com)

49. Tuck Into a Traditional Sunday Roast at the Cat & Mutton

If you leave London without tucking into a hearty Sunday roast, you simply haven't experienced the real London. If you're not familiar with the Sunday Roast concept, it's basically the lunch that almost everyone in Britain will eat on a Sunday, and it combines some kind of roasted meat with roast potatoes, gravy, Yorkshire puddings (a savoury risen pancake), and various other veggies. Almost every pub in London will lay on a Sunday roast, but we are very fond of the servings at the Cat & Mutton in Hackney. Just be sure to reserve a table because it's always popular.

(76 Broadway Market; www.catandmutton.com)

50. Go Cigar Shopping at James J Fox

While the smoking ban is fully enforced throughout all of the United Kingdom, if you still love to puff on a cigar, somewhere you can go to peruse the best selection of cigars in all of London is a shop called James J Fox in the upscale Mayfair neighbourhood. Here you can buy luxury cigars, smoking tobacco, pipes, and other smoking accessories. If there's nothing to suit you, then perhaps more for the smoking grandfather in your life.

(19 St James's St; www.jjfox.co.uk)

51. Learn How to Bake Bread at E5 Bakehouse

Brits are very fond of baking, and many locals take this pastime very seriously indeed, particularly when it comes to bread making. There are numerous wonderful bakeries dotted around the city, but there's only a few of these that actually offer bread making workshops, and the E5 Bakehouse, located in trendy Hackney, is one of them. You'll learn cool things like how to make a sourdough starter, and loads more. And if you don't fancy a whole day of baking, you should pop in for a sandwich at the very least.

(395 Mentmore Terrace E8; http://e5bakehouse.com)

52. Smell the Roses at Kew Gardens

Yes, London is a bustling city with lots of energy, but many people who haven't been to the city before fail to realise that London is also an incredibly green city with many peaceful spaces for you to relax and unwind, and one of the best of these places is Kew Gardens, on the western outskirts of the city. Now, this is no ordinary botanical garden as it actually contains the largest botanical and mycological collections in the world. Highlights include a treetop walkway, an Alpine House, and a stunning Orangery.

(www.kew.org)

53. Treat Yourself During London Cocktail Week

When you're on holiday, it's the time to treat yourself and indulge. And what screams of indulgence more than a cocktail (or five)? While there's certainly no shortage of hotspots in the capital where can grab a fruity alcoholic beverage, if you're serious about cocktails, you'll really want to maximise your drinking time during London Cocktail Week, which takes place in October each year. During this week, there are special cocktail deals that can be found all over the city, as well as a pop-up cocktail village in the East End.

(https://drinkup.london/cocktailweek)

54. Be Wowed by the Street Art of East London

London is most definitely a very creative city, but you can only get one perspective on the city's arts culture if you hop from one posh gallery to another. The youth culture is also very important in London, and it's the art from the city's young people that you can see all over the city streets, particularly in East London. Of course, you can see this for yourself, but we can also recommend the Shoreditch Street Art Tours that will take you to the best street art spotting locations, and the tours take place every Saturday.

(www.shoreditchstreetarttours.co.uk)

55. Enjoy Some Tranquillity at the London Buddhist Centre

London is a city full of action, but at times this mean that the British capital can be a tad overwhelming. If you find yourself in London with a need to centre yourself, the London Buddhist Centre in the Bethnal Green area is a place that you should know about. You can drop in to one of their donation-only meditation settings, which take place most days of the week, and if you want to take the practice a little further, you should check out their one day workshops. *(51 Roman Road E2; www.lbc.org.uk)*

56. Watch a Musical on London's West End

London's theatre scene is really incredible. There are lots of different types of performances that can be watched, but if you are into musicals, the West End scene is particularly strong. For the most popular plays it can definitely be a good idea to book your tickets in advance, especially if you want the best seats in the house, but even if you buy a ticket the day before, just make sure that you see a show.

57. Shop for Vintage Threads at Beyond Retro

London is one of the greatest shopping cities on the face of the earth, and the reason for this is because there are stores to cater for all budgets and all tastes. There are the high end shops on Bond Street, the high street shops all over the city, and there's also a great vintage scene, particularly in the East End. Beyond Retro have two shops in the East End, one in Dalston and one by Brick Lane, and both are incredible for finding reasonably priced vintage treasures. Sometimes they even have live music gigs inside as well.

(110-112 Cheshire St E2; www.beyondretro.com)

58. Tuck Into a Big Ol' Plate of Fish n Chips

If there is one food that you think of being traditionally British, it's probably fish and chips, and a trip to London would not be complete without tucking into a plate of all that deliciousness. There are fish and chips shops dotted all over the city, but our favourite of the bunch might just be Fish House, which is located just outside of picturesque Victoria Park. The chips are chunky, the fish is soft, and the batter is crispy – and on a sunny day, the perfect location means you can eat your plateful in the park.

(128 Lauriston Road E9; www.fishhouse.co.uk)

59. Meet the Animals at Hackney City Farm

The city farm movement is pretty popular in London, but there's one city farm that was doing its thing long before it was trendy to do so. Hackney City Farm is located in Hipster Central, but walk through the gates of the farm and you'll enter into a totally different world. Farmyard animals on the farm include goats, chickens, ducks, donkeys, rabbits, and

guinea pigs. If you're travelling with kids, this is a great place to come, pet the animals, and connect with nature.
(http://hackneycityfarm.co.uk)

60. Watch the Annual Pantomime at Hackney Empire

Hackney Empire is one of the most renowned stages in all of London. Throughout the year, you can catch all kinds of events at this theatre, including contemporary music gigs, stand up comedy shows, and more. But one of our highlights of the annual programme of events has to be the pantomime, which is staged at Christmas time. Pantomimes in Britain are fun, family friendly shows that tell classic tales such as Aladdin and Red Riding Hood.
(291 Mare Street E8; https://hackneyempire.co.uk)

61. Get a Caffeine Kick at the London Coffee Festival

If you are the kind of person who can't function in the morning without your first cup of coffee, you might be a little wary about visiting a tea drinking nation. But there is no need to fear, particularly if you visit London for its annual London

Coffee Festival. Taking place in April each year, the London Coffee Festival is the ultimate destination for a powerful caffeine boost. At the festival, you'll find exciting events like food and coffee pairings, latte art workshops, and even espresso martini parties.

(www.londoncoffeefestival.com)

62. Scale the Roof of the O2 Arena

When major international music artists come to London, there is one venue where they are sure to play, and that is the O2 Arena in the east part of the city. But many people don't realise that there's way more to do at this arena than just watching concerts. And for all outdoor adventurers, something you shouldn't skip is the opportunity to scale the dome of the arena. The highest point is 52 metres, and you can see for 15 miles around when you are at the peak.

(Peninsula Square SE10; www.theo2.co.uk)

63. Take a Tour of the Beefeater Distillery

Head to any beer garden in the summer time, and as well as plenty of pints of lager, you will also see people sipping on refreshing gin and tonics. Gin is endlessly popular in Britain, and one way to get under the skin of the British gin culture is to visit the Beefeater Distillery. This distillery only opened its doors to the public in 2014, so it's still something of a secret on the tourist scene. You'll learn all about gin's history in London, the history of the Beefeater brand, and, of course, you'll get to sip on some of the good stuff.

(20 Montford Pl SE11; http://beefeaterdistillery.com)

64. Forage for Goodies at the Bermondsey Antiques Market

If you have yet to do your souvenir shopping in London, and you would like to avoid the cheesy branded t-shirts from overpriced souvenir shops, somewhere you could go to find something really exceptional to take home with you is the Bermondsey Antiques market. This market only opens on Friday mornings, and when it comes to grabbing something really special, the early bird certainly catches the worm. In fact, the traders start setting up at 4am, and it's a good idea to be there at 5am to find the best pieces.

(Bermondsey Square SE1; https://bermondseysquare.net/bermondsey-antiques-market)

65. Catch a Music Concert in the Round at Roundhouse

The UK has made an incredible splash on the music scene, from the Beatles to Adele, and One Direction to the Rolling stones. And so it should come as no surprise that there are many music venues to be found all over the capital, and cool gigs to attend on every night of the week. One of the coolest music venues in the capital is the Roundhouse, where most of the concerts are actually staged in the round for a far more immersive experience.

(Chalk Farm Rd NW1; www.roundhouse.org.uk)

66. Watch the Sunrise on Hampstead Heath

Hampstead Heath might just be the most iconic green space in the whole of the city, and it's a must visit for any outdoorsy type. On Hampstead Heath, you can explore more than 320 hectares of green land, and with many rollicking hills throughout the park, it's also a great place to get a work out in. Parliament Hill is a very special part of Hampstead Heath, and it's where many people go to watch the sun rise as there is a fantastic view of all of London on a clear day.

67. Enjoy a Perfect Breakfast at Balthazar Boulangerie

As the saying goes, breakfast is the most important meal of the day, but with so many dining options strewn across the British capital it can be difficult to know where's the best place to start your day of eating. Well, we think that the Balthazar Boulangerie, a fancy bakery in the centre of the city, is a very special place indeed. They serve up an incredible Full English with all the trimmings for £15, and we can't think of any better way to get the day off to a flying start.

(4-6 Russell Street; http://balthazarlondon.com/boulangerie)

68. Watch a Movie Marathon at the Prince Charles Cinema

While it's true that London is a city that is brimming full of exciting sights and attractions, there are days when all you want to do is catch a movie. When that moment arises, head straight for the Prince Charles Cinema in Leicester Square. This is one of the cheapest cinemas in the city, and they also have special events. We love their all night movie marathons, with themes such as classic Arnie movies and horror movie specials.

(7 Leicester Pl; https://princecharlescinema.com)

69. Take a Day Trip to Beautiful Windsor Castle

London is a very large city, and it's well worth exploring the outer reaches of the city. Just outside of the city, there is a rather upscale area called Windsor, and it's here that you can find the majestic Windsor Castle. For history buffs, this castle is a must visit, as it dates way back to the 11th century and the Norman times. The highlight of walking through the castle has to be the State Apartments, which date to the 19th century and are the very definition of opulence.

70. Swig on Beers at UBREW

Something that you'll notice fairly swiftly on your trip to London is that the Brits are more than a little bit fond of the occasional pint of beer. Of course, pop your head into any pub and you'll be served some of the standard European beers, but there are also some awesome microbrewery and craft beer places to check out. UBREW in South London might be our favourite. As well as serving up delicious beers, they also have beer brewing courses for true beer aficionados. *(29 Old Jamaica Business Estate, 24 Old Jamaica Rd; https://ubrew.cc)*

71. Take Public Transport on the River Thames

One of the most iconic features of London is the channel that cuts it completely in half, the River Thames. There are many wonderful ways of exploring this river. You can take picturesque walks at dusk along the Southbank, or perhaps you'd like to enjoy a formal dinner cruise. Something that few visitors to London comprehend is that there is actually public boat transportation along the River Thames as well. You can pay for tickets using your Oyster Card, and see all the majesty of the Thames from on top of the water.

72. Eat the Best Burger of Your Life at Mac & Wild

Okay, so the likelihood is that you haven't travelled all the way to London just to eat burgers, but let's face it, sometimes it's only a burger that will do. And when that moment strikes, the place to go is Mac & Wild, a restaurant that actually specialises in game and seafood from the Scottish Highlands. The Venimoo Burger is something extra special. Combining a beef patty, a venison patty, béarnaise cheese, and caramelised onions inside a soft brioche bun, this is the Daddy of all burgers in London.

(65 Great Titchfield St, Fitzrovia; www.macandwild.com)

73. Be Totally Stunned by Westminster Abbey

Prepare to be mesmerised by all of the stunning church architecture that you can find around the city. And if it's church architecture that really gets you going, you might need to prepare your heart for the sight of Westminster Abbey, a gorgeous gothic abbey that mainly dates back to the 16th century. The abbey has also played a significant role in British history as many monarchs have had their coronation there, and 16 Royal marriages have taken place there too, including the marriage of William and Kate.

(20 Deans Yard; www.westminster-abbey.org)

74. Rock Out in the London Sunshine for Field Day

If you have a penchant for rock and indie music, you need to get your tickets for Field Day Festival sooner rather than later. This yearly festival takes place each year in August, and while most other day festivals cater to dance and electronica fans, this festival is very rock oriented. Acts that have performed at Field Day in the past include Mumford & Sons, PJ Harvey, and James Blake.

(http://fielddayfestivals.com)

75. Shop for Beautiful Things at Liberty

London is a beautiful city full of beautiful things, and you can find an abundance of the most beautiful things imaginable at an iconic department store called Liberty. Housed within a stunning Tudor revival building in the centre of the city, Liberty is particularly celebrated for its original graphic prints, which are used on many objects including luxury stationary, beautiful garments, and the highest quality silk scarves. Anything purchased from Liberty will be a souvenir to cherish forever.

(Regent St; www.libertylondon.com)

76. Tuck Into Seafood at Hawksmoor Air Street

One of the benefits of visiting a small island like the UK is that you are never far from the coast, and that means there is incredible seafood everywhere, including London, which isn't actually on the coast. There's an abundance of yummy seafood restaurants in the capital, and we are particularly taken by Hawksmoor Air Street. The highlight of the menu has to be the Brixham Fish Pie with haddock, turbot, and monkfish inside. Any seafood lover will be in fish heaven.

(5 Air Street, Piccadilly; http://thehawksmoor.com/locations/airstreet)

77. Take a Grizzly Trip to Hyde Park Pet Cemetery

A day trip to a cemetery probably isn't going to be at the very top of your to do list, but trust us when we say that this cemetery is unlike any other you've visited as it's totally dedicated to pets from London. The pet cemetery is tucked away in the corner to the west of Hyde Park, and it was opened in 1881 by a kindly groundskeeper, and pets were buried there until 1903. Somehow, seeing the tiny gravestones gives us the awwwz instead of making us feel creeped out.

78. Have a Tea Filled Afternoon at Urban Tea Rooms

It's no secret that the British are rather fond of a cup of tea, and we predict that you'll be drinking more tea than you've ever drank before on your trip to London. If you really want to amp up your tea experience in the capital, heading to one of the many tearooms is a stellar plan. The Urban Tea Rooms is unbeatable on every level. There are many types of loose leaf tea on offer, some delicious eats, and in the evening time you can even treat yourself to a tea flavoured cocktail.
(19 Kingly Street, Carnaby; http://urbantearooms.com)

79. See Freud's Couch Up Close

Although the world famous neurologist Sigmund Freud was born in Austria, he spent the last year of his life in London with his family. That same home that he lived in in the 1930s has is now where you can find the Freud Museum. The Freuds moved all of their household objects to this London home, and you can still see them there today, with pieces like 18th century Austrian country furniture. The star of the show, however, is always the psychoanalytic couch, which had been given to him by one of his patients.

(20 Marsefield Gardens NW3; www.freud.org.uk)

80. Visit a Masterpiece of Art Deco Design, Eltham Palace

Eltham Palace is one of the most unique heritage sites in the British capital. This unoccupied Royal palace has its origins in the early 14th century. It was in the 1930s that the palace was passed on to owners with a very different style, and the Great Hall was renovated with a beautiful art deco style. The combination of all the historic styles through to the art deco period is really what makes this a unique spot in London. There's also 19 acres of beautiful gardens to explore, and a working bridge over the palace moat.

(Court Yard, Eltham; www.english-heritage.org.uk/visit/places/eltham-palace-and-gardens)

81. Watch Some Up and Coming Theatre at Battersea Arts Centre

London is an arts city through and through, and there is something for every kind of arts lover in the capital. If you would prefer to forego a trip to a grand opera house, and instead you'd like a better idea of the up and coming arts scene in London, a great place to check out some work is the Battersea Arts Centre. You can find all kinds of performance work here, but all of it is by young, independent companies who put on really interesting performances. The prices are also great if you're on a budget.

(Lavender Hill SW11; www.bac.org.uk)

82. Sip on Pimms During Wimbledon

As well as being a cultural city, London is also a sporty city at times, and this is never more evident than during the annual Wimbledon tennis event, which takes place every summer. We'll be straight with you, getting tickets for these tennis matches is certainly not easy, but this doesn't mean that you can't join in with the fun. In fact, there are often parks throughout London that erect big screens. And, of course, the thing to munch on while watching the tennis is strawberries and cream washed down with a glass of refreshing Pimms.

(www.wimbledon.com)

83. Drink in a Secret Underground Tube Bar

There's certainly no shortage of places where you can grab a swift drink in London, but one of the most special of them all simply has to be a bar called Cahoots. Located in Kingly Court in central London, enter Cahoots and you'll be transported back in time to the Blitz. The bar also has an Underground theme, so it brings all the best things about London together in one place. And the electro swing music really gets things going each night.

(13 Kingly Court, Carnaby; https://cahoots-london.com)

84. Go Bird Watching at the London Wetland Centre

The London Wetland Centre is one of the most recent additions to the capital's outdoorsy scene, and it was opened in the year 2000 by Sir David Attenborough. This nature reserve was formed from four disused Victorian reservoirs, and there are 105 species of birds that live there, so it's the perfect spot for a bit of bird watching on a sunny day. Inside there's wading birds like redshanks and lapwings, warblers like sedge warblers, as well as beauties like kingfishers, sparrow hawks, and sand martins.

(Queen Elizabeth's Walk, Barnes; www.wwt.org.uk/wetland-centres/london)

85. Laze the Days Away at Camden Beach

One negative about London is that during the summer months there is no beach to enjoy. Or is there? In fact, during those months, the Roundhouse music venue in Camden transforms its bar and terrace area into a city beach. The venue does a really great job of creating a British beach environment with tonnes of real sand, deck chairs, buckets and spades, and beach BBQs and cocktails so you won't have to fear going hungry or thirsty.

(Chalk Farm Rd NW1; www.roundhouse.org.uk)

86. Tuck Into a Doner Kebab After a Drunken Night on the Town

Every country in the world has its own variety of drunk food, and as the Brits are very much into social drinking, we reckon it's quite possible that you'll be indulging in some of these late night noms. There are many varieties of drunk food you can devour in the capital, but the most popular of them all is the doner kebab. These kebabs are actually Turkish, and you can find them in many Turkish kebab shops, but doners have actually become so mainstream that you can even find them in fish and chip shops, and fried chicken joints as well.

87. Dance, Dance, Dance at Eastern Electrics

Dance music fans will have an awesome time on a trip to London, but the best of London's dance scene isn't only found in nightclubs but also on the festival circuit. Eastern Electrics, an annual summer dance festival hosted in Hatfield House is relatively new to the city's festival circuit, and yet it's already winning awards. Big names such as Groove Armada and Skream have already played, and the festival is only going to become more popular in the coming years. *(www.easternelectrics.com)*

88. Feel Floral at Columbia Road Flower Market

Market culture is something very important in London, and you can find different markets for different purposes. Columbia Road Flower Market is enduringly popular, and one of the most vibrant markets in the city. This market takes place every Sunday, and the whole city overflows with the most incredible colours, and the scents of the various flowers. As the market is in the heart of the East End, there are many options for Sunday lunch in a local pub nearby as well. *(www.columbiaroad.info)*

89. Relax in the Stunning Wellcome Library Reading Room

Everybody knows about London's main sights and attractions, but one of the loveliest things about this city is that there are hidden nooks that even many local people don't know about. There are so many libraries in London, and many of these are certainly special spaces, and we are particularly enamoured by the Wellcome Library Reading Room, which has a carefully selected collection of books and artefacts about the human condition. A wonderful place for pondering.

(183 Euston Rd, Kings Cross; https://wellcomelibrary.org)

90. Eat the Best Chinese Food of Your Life at Hakkasan

Okay, the chances are that you are probably not in London to eat Chinese food, but if you pay a visit to Michelin star Chinese restaurant Hakkasan, you'll no doubt want to eat there on every night of your stay in the city. Now, this is not the Chinese food next to the bus station all you can eat restaurant, but something way more special. How about Australian lobster with spicy black bean sauce and crisp noodles, or the langoustines wrapped in vermicelli noodles with a garlic and rice wine sauce? We are salivating thinking about it.

(17 Bruton Street, Mayfair; http://hakkasan.com)

91. Embrace Your Inner Child at the Museum of Childhood

If you're a museum lover, London is a city that will not disappoint. This city has an incredible array of museums, and a good number of them are free to enter, but when scouting for museums don't just stick to the city centre. Venture into the east, and you'll find the Museum of Childhood in Bethnal Green. This museum has a very well put together selection of artefacts relating to children's lives, from toys from years gone by to artefacts from schools.

(Cambridge Heath Road E2; www.vam.ac.uk/moc)

92. Go Gin Crazy at the London Gin Club

Londoners love a tipple on any night of the week, but it's gin that always rules the roost in London Town. If you want to know what all the fuss is about, the London Gin Club is where you can get schooled. This bar in central London specialises, as you might have guessed, in gin, and serves up more than 130 varieties of the spirit, as well as decadent gin cocktails. And for those really serious about gin, the gin tasting menu of either 4 or 8 samples is totally the way to go.

(22 Great Chapel Street, Soho; https://thelondonginclub.com)

93. Show Off Your Singing Skills at Lucky Voice

You don't need to have the vocal acrobatics of Mariah Carey to enjoy a karaoke night, and the most iconic place for karaoke in London is Lucky Voice. At Lucky Voice, you book a booth by the hour and cram in as many friends as you possibly can. There's a dress up box with wigs, glasses, and other silly things, and the songlist is second to none. What's more, there are branches all over London, so there's bound to be one close to where you are staying.

(www.luckyvoice.com)

94. Learn How to Make Chocolate Treats at Paxton Chocolate

Who doesn't love chocolate? Only very very silly people indeed. You're not one of them, and that's why you need to know about Paxton Chocolate, located in the East End's Bethnal Green. This chocolatier sells some of the yummiest treats in London, but they go one better by hosting workshops teaching you how to make them yourself. You'll learn how to make your very own chocolate truffles, and it's a skill you can take away with you and use forever.

(38 Cheshire Street E2; www.paxtonchocolate.com)

95. Have Some Belly Laughs at Soho Theatre

London has a fantastic stand-up comedy scene, and one place that we go to again and again for belly laughs is the Soho Theatre. This theatre in central London is not only a stage for comedians, but we think that makes the comedy shows here that much more interesting. You might have comedy combined with drag, or comedy combined into more of a story-telling narrative. There's something to see here on every night of the week so do keep up to date with their programme of events.

(21 Dean Street, Soho; www.sohotheatre.com)

96. Take the Jack the Ripper Tour of Whitechapel

In the late 19th century, prostitutes working on the streets of East London were singled out by a serial killer who is still unidentified to this day, but who goes by the name of Jack the Ripper. If you'd like to know more about this grizzly figure and his effect on the capital, you should absolutely take the Jack the Ripper Walking Tour, which will walk you through the streets of Whitechapel where the murders took place.

(www.thejacktherippertour.com)

97. Watch a Movie With Cocktails at The Electric

There are times, even when you're in an exciting place like London, that the only thing you want to do is kick back and watch a great movie. When that moment strikes, don't just go to any old cinema but the Electric cinema in Shoreditch. This place is way more than just a cinema, it offers a total experience. You'll feel as comfortable as ever in their leather armchairs and wrapped in cashmere blankets, and you'll have your own little table to hold the cocktails of your choosing. *(64-66 Redchurch St; www.electriccinema.co.uk/shoreditch)*

98. Take a Life-Changing Class at the School of Life

Let's face it, life isn't always a breeze. The contemporary philosopher, Alain de Botton, totally gets that, and his school is dedicated to providing pragmatic philosophy for the masses. The School of Life offers one off classes and workshops that can help you out in all kinds of areas. Perhaps you'd like to know how to find meaningful work, maybe you would like to have better conversations, and maybe you'd like help facing your own mortality. There's classes in these subjects and more, as well as a great bookshop on-site.

99. Enjoy a Summer Barbecue on London Fields

One of the really cool things about London is that you can eat and drink outside without any problem, so you'll never get cuffed by the police for swigging from a can of beer on the street. In reality, this means that when the sun shines down on London, everyone descends upon local parks with disposable barbecues and cans of cider. A very popular spot for this is London Fields, a lovely spot in the East End. This makes for a fun and cheap afternoon in the sun.

(70 Marchmont St, Kings Cross; www.theschooloflife.com)

100. Learn How to Cook at the Bourne & Hollingsworth Kitchen

While London certainly doesn't have the most acclaimed foodie credentials of any city in the world, we don't think that you'll be disappointed by the food there, and there's also a few places where you can learn to cook great food from renowned chefs. The Bourne & Hollingsworth kitchen has regular cooking classes that are always mega exciting. How about learning how to make sausages from scratch, or maybe you'd enjoy a knife skills class?

(42 Northampton Road EC1R; www.bandhkitchen.com)

101. Party in the Street for Notting Hill Carnival

Ever since 1966, the West Indian community has led a massive street party on the streets of Notting Hill called the Notting Hill carnival. This honestly might be the most fun weekend of the entire calendar year in London, as everybody is very welcome to join in with all the fun. Whether you want to dance on the street in the day time or party right throughout the night, you're very welcome to join in as little or as much as you would like.

(http://www.thelondonnottinghillcarnival.com)

Before You Go...

Thanks for reading **101 Coolest Things to Do in London**. We hope that it makes your trip a memorable one!

Keep your eyes peeled on <u>www.101coolestthings.com</u>, and have an incredible time in the British capital.

Team 101 Coolest Things

30072675R00033

Printed in Great Britain
by Amazon